WOLVERINE and the X-MEN ALPHA & OMEGA

WRITER: **BRIAN WOOD**

ART (WESTCHESTER): **ROLAND BOSCHI** & **DAN BROWN**

ART (CONSTRUCT): **MARK BROOKS** WITH **ANDREW CURRIE**, **JAY LEISTEN**, **NORMAN LEE**, **RONDA PATTISON**, **WALDEN WONG**, **ANDRES MOSSA** & **CAM SMITH**

LETTERER: **VC'S JOE SABINO**

COVER ART: **MARK BROOKS** (#1-2) & **JOHN TYLER CHRISTOPHER** (#3-4)

ASSISTANT EDITOR: **SEBASTIAN GIRNER** • EDITOR: **JEANINE SCHAEFER**
GROUP EDITOR: **NICK LOWE**

COLLECTION EDITOR: **JENNIFER GRÜNWALD**
ASSISTANT EDITORS:
ALEX STARBUCK & **NELSON RIBEIRO**
EDITOR, SPECIAL PROJECTS: **MARK D. BEAZLEY**
SENIOR EDITOR, SPECIAL PROJECTS:
JEFF YOUNGQUIST
SENIOR VICE PRESIDENT OF SALES: **DAVID GABRIEL**
SVP OF BRAND PLANNING & COMMUNICATIONS:
MICHAEL PASCIULLO
BOOK DESIGN: **RODOLFO MURAGUCHI** & **JEFF POWELL**

EDITOR IN CHIEF:
AXEL ALONSO
CHIEF CREATIVE OFFICER:
JOE QUESADA
PUBLISHER:
DAN BUCKLEY
EXECUTIVE PRODUCER:
ALAN FINE

WOLVERINE and the X-MEN
ALPHA & OMEGA

Born with incredible telepathic powers and a rebellious nature, Quentin Quire has caused no small amount of trouble for a teenage boy, from inciting riots to declaring a full-on war on humanity. His most recent antics have caused Wolverine to attempt to set him straight by forcefully enrolling him in the recently reopened mutant school in Westchester. But Quentin despises Wolverine and has vowed revenge...

YOU *GOT* TO BE KIDDING ME. WHO SPARS AT SEVEN IN THE MORNING?

WHAT AM I SAYING? *SADISTS* LIKE LOGAN DO, DUH.

MR. QUIRE?

SIGH...YES, RACHEL?

"MS. GREY" WILL DO NICELY, THANK YOU.

YOUR PSYCHWAR 101 CLASS STARTED NINETY SECONDS AGO.

YEAH, I KNOW, I'M LISTENING IN.

BESIDES, I SHOULD BE TEACHING THAT CLASS. "PSYCHWAR 101"? MAYBE WHEN I WAS *SIX YEARS OLD* I COULD'VE LEARNED SOMETHING THERE.

ALONG WITH SOME BASIC MANNERS, APPARENTLY.

GET TO CLASS, QUENTIN. NOW.

PEASANTS, ALL OF THEM.

"PSYCHWAR"... THEY WOULDN'T KNOW A PSYCHWAR IF IT WALKED UP AND KICKED THEIR ASS.

SPEAKING OF WHICH...

LOGAN!

WHUMP

WHAT THE HELL 'RE YOU DOING?

I--

LET ME UP!

FORGIVE THE MENTAL INTRUSION. I PROMISE YOU I'M NOT PRYING. LIKE, IN A SKEEVY WAY.

IT'S NOT REALLY ABOUT YOU, ICHIKI.

A DAY OFF OF SCHOOL, A NICE SLEEP-IN, CATCH UP ON YOUR BEAUTY REST OR WHATEVER.

WHEN YOU THINK ABOUT IT, I'M REALLY DOING YOU A FAVOR. I'M DOING ALL OF US A FAVOR. I THINK IT'S TIME FOR THE STUDENTS TO FLEX A LITTLE MUSCLE AROUND HERE, FIGHT THE POWER, AM I RIGHT?

YEAH, THAT'S A SHOT AT YOU, YOU NEANDERTHAL. DEAL WITH IT.

...LOGAN...

?

QUENTIN QUIRE!

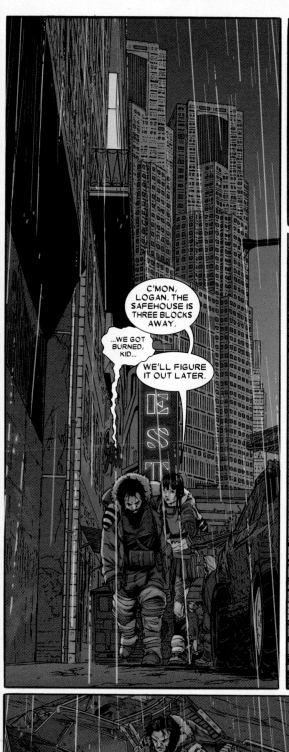

C'MON, LOGAN. THE SAFEHOUSE IS THREE BLOCKS AWAY.

...WE GOT BURNED, KID...

WE'LL FIGURE IT OUT LATER.

HOW DID YOU TAKE THAT HIT AND SURVIVE...?

HOW DID YOU?

I THINK WE BOTH HAVE SOME UNANSWERED QUESTIONS.

HOLD UP, YOU NEED SOMETHING TO EAT.

HURRY UP.

HMMM.

LOGAN!

2

7.62-MM SVD DRAGUNOV SNIPER RIFLE.

JUST KEEPING YOU ON YOUR TOES, ARMOR.

QUENTIN! DUDE, YOU *LOOK* LIKE *HELL!*

DID YOU SLEEP AT *ALL* LAST NIGHT?

NAH...

...BUT I CHANGED MY SHIRT.

I HATE PEOPLE

UGH, FORGET IT. I'LL JUST TELL RACHEL I COULDN'T FIND THE BOOK. MAYBE I CAN DOWNLOAD IT ONLINE LATER OR SOMETHING.

AND HEY, QUENTIN? DON'T TAKE THIS THE WRONG WAY...

...BUT YOU COULD USE A SHOWER. JUST SAYING. AS WELL AS A LESSON ON WHEN TO TAKE A HINT.

I GET THAT YOUR VIDEO GAME IS COOL, AND HONESTLY, THERE'S A GIRL OUT THERE WHO WILL BE AS IMPRESSED AS YOU ARE ABOUT IT...

...BUT THAT GIRL IS JUST NOT ME, SORRY.

...
WERE YOU EVER ACTUALLY LISTENING TO ME?

WAS WHO LISTENING?

OH, HI RACHEL.

MS. GREY. GET TO CLASS, QUENTIN.

PLUS, HISAKO.

I HAVE NO BEEF WITH HER. SHE DOESN'T DESERVE TOO MUCH MORE OF THIS.

I CAN *NOT* BELIEVE NO ONE'S IMPRESSED WITH WHAT I'VE BUILT HERE. SHAME TO JUST PULL THE PLUG.

HISAKO? WHAT DOES SHE HAVE TO DO WITH ANYTHING?

I DUNNO WHAT'S GOING ON, BUT I THINK YOU MIGHT HAVE THE *WRONG* IDEA.

ONE LAST BATTLE?

MAYBE I SHOULD GO. I'LL BORROW THOSE CDS LATER...

I ONLY NEED, LIKE, FOUR HOURS SLEEP?

A BIT OF ENHANCED GAMEPLAY SHOULD KEEP THEM ON THE RUN UNTIL THEN. COUPLE CURVEBALLS, A FEW NEW PLAYERS IN THE MIX.

PREDICTIVE A.I...RANDOMIZED MAP DESIGN...NEW ENEMY WEAPON PROFILES... COLLATERAL DAMAGE SAFETIES OFF...

I JUST NEED FOUR HOURS.

YEAH, I'M GONNA GO...

NO!

YOU. STAY HERE.

YOU'RE MY ALARM CLOCK. WAKE ME AT MIDNIGHT.

EXCUSE ME?

CLICK

WHAT THE HELL?

REY SCHOOL
TED YOUNGSTERS

MORNING.

GUH

OH
CRAP!

OW OW
OW OW OW
OW OW OW
OW

3

RESTROOM

WHO AM I KIDDING?

I'VE CROSSED THE RUBICON ON THIS ONE. PAST THE POINT OF CALLING THIS A PRANK.

AND SOMEWHERE OUT THERE IS A WALKING SLAB OF LOGAN'S ID, BAYING FOR MY BLOOD.

SAY WHAT?

TOAD, YOU GOT IT MADE IN THE SHADE, BROTHER.

SAY WHAT AGAIN?

EXACTLY MY POINT.

ON ONE HAND, I HAVE ACHIEVED SO MUCH. IN THE CONSTRUCT, I HAVE CREATED MY SISTINE CEILING. IT'S *GORGEOUS*.

EXCEPT IT'S OUT OF CONTROL AND KILLING LOGAN AND HISAKO.

AND I DON'T KNOW HOW TO TURN IT OFF.

I WONDER IF ALL OMEGA-LEVEL TELEPATHS FEEL SO BURDENED BY OUR EXCELLENCE?

HOW ARE YOU FEELING?

LIKE HELL.

IT'S...NEW. NOT SURE I'D WANT TO REPEAT THE EXPERIENCE, BUT IT'S AN INTERESTING RIDE JUST THE SAME.

TO GET PROGRESSIVELY WORSE.

YEAH, WELL, YOU'RE *WOUNDED,* LOGAN, AND YOU AREN'T GETTING PROPER MEDICAL ATTENTION.

AND THAT'S AN OPTION?

HISAKO, LISTEN. ABOUT WHAT'S HAPPENING OUTSIDE.

YOU MEAN THE *END OF THE WORLD?*

NICE WAY TO PUT IT...

...BECAUSE I DON'T THINK THAT *IS* OUR WORLD.

4

RACHEL?

WHAT IS IT, CHAMBER?

IT'S ARMOR. WE COMPLETED THE HEADCOUNT AND SHE WAS NOT IN HER PANIC ROOM OR ANYWHERE ELSE WE COULD THINK OF.

OH, FANTASTIC.

THANKS. CHECK GATE SECURITY; MAKE SURE SHE DIDN'T EXIT THE GROUNDS.

LOGAN, I PRAY YOU HAD NOTHING TO DO WITH THIS...

"...BECAUSE YOU WOULD NEVER FORGIVE YOURSELF."

PULL IT TOGETHER...DON'T SHOW WEAKNESS, DON'T EXPOSE THE CRACKS...

HERE THEY COME. *STAND STRONG.* KEY WORD: *INTEGRITY.* IT'S NOT A LIE IF *YOU* BELIEVE IT, QUENTIN...

MAKE A MESS, TOAD'LL CLEAN IT UP. OVERFLOW THE TRASH CAN?

BUMP

BUMP

TOAD PICKS IT UP. TREAT SCHOOL LIKE OWN PERSONAL RUBBISH HEAP? WHY NOT.

TOAD'LL-- WHOA!

MS. GREY!

TOAD, WHAT IS IT?

HISAKO, DOWNSTAIRS! SHE'S OKAY!

FIND KARMA. SHE CAN HELP YOU. I'M TIED UP HERE.

YES.

AND WELL DONE, TOAD.

I KNOW!

SO, QUIRE, WE'RE MUTANTS, EH? WEIRDLY, I KNOW WHAT THAT IS.

HISAKO'S GOT THAT ARMOR, I HAVE THESE. ANYTHING ELSE?

YOU HAVE ACCELERATED HEALING POWERS.

WHUMP

WHUMP

WHUMP

I DO?

YEAH, BUT I, UH, DISABLED THAT A LITTLE BIT.

I HATE YOUR GUTS.

BELIEVE ME, I KNOW.

HEADS UP, STREET AHEAD!

HEY, CAN YOU BRING THAT BUILDING BACK?

I HAVE IT IN MY BUFFERS. WATCH OUT...

MMMMMMMMMMMP

WHOA, THAT WAS COOLER THAN I THOUGHT IT WOULD BE.

ENJOYING YOURSELF, YOU LITTLE *FASCIST?*

WE CAN KEEP RUNNING, BUT EVENTUALLY THEY'LL GET US.

WE GOTTA CUT ALL THIS OFF AT THE SOURCE.

...

I'M *TRYING!*

TRY A LITTLE FASTER...

...I'LL HOLD THEM OFF.

AND SEE WHAT YOU CAN DO ABOUT THAT HEALING FACTOR!

SO WHEREVER WE'RE REALLY FROM, ARE WE, LIKE, FRIENDS?

I DON'T REALLY HAVE FRIENDS.

OH.

HOLD ON. I THINK I GOT HIS HEALING FACTOR SWITCHED BACK ON.

YOU "THINK"? YOU DESIGNED ALL OF THIS, SO WHY IS IT SO HARD FOR YOU TO CONTROL?

WELL, IF YOU ASKED ME YESTERDAY, I'D SAY SOMETHING LIKE, IT'S JUST SO WELL MADE THAT IT TOOK ON A LIFE OF ITS OWN.

BUT MORE LIKELY IT'S BECAUSE I'M A MESS AND I DON'T HAVE A HANDLE ON MY TELEPATHY LIKE I THOUGHT I DID.

SO WHY DO ALL THOSE SOLDIERS HAVE MY DEAD BROTHER'S FACE?

I--I DIDN'T KNOW--

THE CONSTRUCT, IT DRAWS ON YOUR MEMORIES AS MUCH AS MINE... LOGAN'S TOO...I DON'T EVEN KNOW WHAT YOUR BROTHER LOOKS LIKE. LOOK, THIS IS REALLY HARD--

SAVE IT.

I'M NOT GONNA FEEL BAD FOR YOU. JUST GET US SOMEPLACE SAFE.

LOOK NEXT TO YOU. YOU'LL SEE A BUTTON.

5

BAM BAM

QUIRE

QUENTIN QUIRE! OPEN UP!

LISTEN, QUENTIN, THIS HAS--

! WHAT WAS THAT?

THAT... HURT.

QUIRE, I AM GOING TO TAKE YOU APART--

KRASH

+GASP+

...HISAKO!

RACHEL, HISAKO'S AWAKE!

STAY THERE, I'M ON MY WAY.

OH MY GOD, HISAKO, WHAT HAPPENED TO YOU?

...

WHERE'S QUENTIN QUIRE?

QUENTIN?

EW, WHY DO YOU CARE?

"HEH."

TALK ABOUT *PSYCHWAR 101.*

X: THE END.

#1 2ND PRINTING VARIANT BY JIM CHEUNG

KID OMEGA

REAL NAME: Quentin Quire
ALIASES: Top Boss
IDENTITY: Publicly known
OCCUPATION: Student, anarchist, terrorist; former gang leader
CITIZENSHIP: USA
PLACE OF BIRTH: Unrevealed
KNOWN RELATIVES: Unidentified adoptive parents
GROUP AFFILIATION: Jean Grey School for Higher Learning student body; formerly Omega Gang, Xavier Institute student body
EDUCATION: Various high school courses at Jean Grey School for Higher Learning and Xavier Institute for Higher Learning
FIRST APPEARANCE: (Photograph) New X-Men #126 (2002); (identified) New X-Men #134 (2003)

HISTORY: Telepathic Quentin Quire was one of the most promising students at the Xavier Institute for Higher Learning, having been inspired by Professor Charles Xavier's dream of peaceful human/mutant integration when he was 13 years old. As a student, Quire created anti-gravity floating devices to grant mobility to the disembodied brain of his fellow student Martha Johansson, longed to be popular and powerful, and became infatuated with fellow student Sophie, one of the telepathic Stepford Cuckoos quintet, hive mind clones of telepathic faculty member Emma Frost. However, the Cuckoos regarded him as a creepy rival

for Xavier's attention and rejected all efforts by Quire to gain Sophie's affections. He regularly carried the front page of a Daily Bugle newspaper released on the day he was born which featured an article on the emergence of mutantkind and an accompanying illustration that depicted mutants as striped shirt-wearing, whip wielding masters of humanity, an image Quire came to regard as a pop-art masterpiece.

Devastated by learning that he was adopted, and haunted by both the extermination of 16 million mutants in the mutant nation of Genosha and the murder of renowned mutant fashion designer and nightclub entrepreneur Jumbo Carnation during an apparent anti-mutant hate crime, Quire began to doubt Xavier's teachings, and developed a more negative and hostile view of the world and of humankind; Quire was unaware Carnation actually died from a self-administered dose of neuro-toxic designer drug Hypercortisone D (aka "Kick"), which increased superhuman mutant powers but also altered the brain's metabolism, greatly enhancing intellectual capacity and imagination but also apparently disengaging inhibitions and rationale. In his frustration at not being able to avenge Carnation, during a musical performance benefit for Carnation Quire disrupted the illusion supposedly handsome and charismatic student Slick (Quincy Marrow) created to hide his misshapen true form, humiliating him in front of the student body, an event that disturbed Xavier. Simultaneously, when blood work revealed Quire's brain was burning sugar at fifteen times faster than normal, the Institute staff became concerned Quire was experiencing a secondary mutation.

WITH OMEGA GANG

Art by Frank Quitely

Around this time, an increasingly arrogant Quire began using Kick and drastically altered his appearance to match the Daily Bugle illustration of mutants, which greatly concerned Xavier, who believed Quentin's attire and aggression would help undermine Xavier's life's reconciliation work with humans. Largely to impress Sophie, Quire assembled a group of students that

OMEGA GANG SYMBOL/TATTOO

Art by Frank Quitely

shared his frustrations and named them the Omega Gang. This group also changed their appearance, got matching tattoos and while regularly using Kick, violently attacked members of the mutant organ-harvesting U-Men and humans they suspected of being anti-mutant, and spray painting the gang's symbol wherever they went. On campus, the Gang assaulted Xavier and rendered him powerless with a helmet based on Magneto (Max Eisenhardt)'s telepathy resistant technology, then during the Institute's Open Day, an event welcoming humans on campus, the Gang fomented a student riot that resulted in at least one student death. While Xavier's mutant emergency response X-Men easily defeated the Omega Gang, Sophie consumed a dose of "Kick" and utilized the X-Men's psychic-enhancement technology to magnify her sisters' telepathic powers to a level higher than Quire's. Though they defeated Quire, Sophie apparently died from the strain.

Possibly triggered by his Kick use, Quire's physical form underwent his secondary mutation and discorporated, leaving him a disembodied consciousness in a containment unit while the remaining members of the Omega Gang were incarcerated in human prisons. Later, when the cosmic avatar known as the Phoenix Force returned to Earth, its

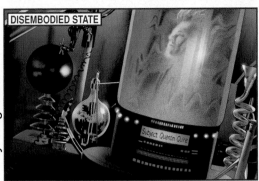

DISEMBODIED STATE

Art by Greg Land

AS TOP BOSS

Art by Mark Brooks

from learning peaceful methods of cohabitation. During the attack, Quire secretly used his telepathy to calm Kilgore's genetic duplicate of the X-Men's sentient island foe Krakoa; discovering the Krakoa duplicate was as lonely and misunderstood as Quire himself privately felt, he encouraged it to request becoming the school's grounds and a member of the X-Men. Within the first week of school, Quire attempted at least 14 militant uprisings, including a small riot in the lunchroom over "draconian dietary restrictions regarding tater-tots," and his lack of personal hygiene and his acidic personality further alienated him from the student body, resulting in his further lashing out at his fellow students.

presence influenced Quire to reconstitute himself in a new physical form, but Quire became distraught when he recalled Sophie's death. He exhumed her corpse and sought out the Phoenix Force to help resurrect her, opposing the X-Men, who sought to contain the dangerous Force to prevent potential destruction it could cause. During the ensuing clash, the Force granted Quire's wish by resurrecting Sophie. However, upon seeing Quire, a disgusted Sophie chose instead to return to death; a heartbroken Quire resumed his disembodied state. When the Institute was destroyed and the X-Men relocated their operations to San Francisco, California, Quire's containment unit was also taken there.

SCHOOL UNIFORM

Art by Chris Bachalo

Quire's consciousness later learned of the X-Men's establishment of an informal mutant nation on the artificial island of Utopia. Believing the idea was originally his, Quire sought to destroy Utopia, but was prevented from doing so by telepaths Martha Johansson and the Stepford Cuckoos. Later, would-be mogul and pre-teen genius Kade Kilgore, while seeking to obtain business for his weapons manufacturing holdings by stoking humanity's fear of mutants, secretly freed Quire from his containment unit and enabled his assault on an international arms control conference in Switzerland, where X-Men leader Cyclops (Scott Summers) was presenting a speech on the danger of mutant-hunting Sentinel technology. Continuing to seek mutant revolution, Quire mentally forced numerous attending world leaders to confess their corrupt or unethical behaviors on live television then publicly claimed credit for his actions; the resulting arms sales greatly pleased Kilgore, but caused anti-mutant chaos worldwide. When arrogantly seeking asylum on Utopia after becoming Earth's most wanted mutant, Quire was detained by the X-Men, and following a philosophical schism that divided the X-Men, Quire was forced by Wolverine (Logan/James Howlett) to attend his newly opened Jean Grey School for Higher Education on the site of the destroyed Xavier Institute in New York state. Despite vocal opposition to Quire's freedom voiced by the Director of US superhuman affairs Captain America (Steve Rogers), Wolverine was allowed to retain Quire in one last effort to reform him on the conditions that Wolverine file weekly updates of Quire's progress, that Quire was monitored by psychic X-Man Marvel Girl (Rachel Grey) and at the first sign of trouble, the Avengers, Earth's premier superhumans, take him into custody.

On the first day of school, during the New York State Department of Education's inspection of the campus, Quire was placed on detention and guarded by headmistress Kitty Pryde's friend Lockheed the dragon to prevent him from causing problems in front of the inspectors. However, to protect his interests in having humankind hate mutantkind, Kilgore and his allies attempted to destroy the school to prevent students

Later, seeking revenge on Wolverine for forcing him to attend the school, Quire extracted his favorite parts from video games he had played and movies he had seen to create a hyper-detailed imaginary world within his brain called the Construct. After he trapped Wolverine's and fellow student Armor (Hisako Ichicki)'s consciousnesses within this world, Quire bragged about it to other students to gain their respect, but he was rejected. However, bereft of Wolverine's psyche, which was living the life of a black market runner that had fallen in his employer's bad graces within the Construct, Wolverine's body was taken over by the animalistic bloodlust that was usually restrained by Wolverine's conscious efforts and went on a rampage within the school while hunting Quire. Realizing his subconscious was helping the Construct take on a life of its own while he slept, Quire entered the Construct and installed himself as the Top Boss of this world while seeking a way to discontinue it from within. As the Boss, Quire convinced Wolverine and Armor to work with him in battling his subconscious, but when all efforts to shut the Construct down failed, Quire realized he had to die to end the program and directed Wolverine to stab him in the heart, a sacrificial act that restored their consciousnesses to their rightful bodies. Following this, a remorseful Quire planned to leave the school to be incarcerated by the Avengers, but impressed by what Quire accomplished with the Construct, Wolverine refused to let him leave and scheduled weekly psychic training sessions with Quire to train Wolverine how to prevent being defeated by similar psychic attacks.

HEIGHT: 5'8"   **EYES:** Brown
WEIGHT: 129 lbs.   **HAIR:** Brown (often dyed pink)

ABILITIES/ACCESSORIES: Quentin Quire is an Omega-level telepath who can form and organize thoughts at the rate of ten million per second. Among his array of mental talents, Quire can communicate telepathically over long distances, read the minds and manipulate the thoughts and bodily functions of others, shield his mind against telepathic probes, remove the consciousnesses of others from their minds, and create entire worlds within his own brain. Quire has demonstrated some telekinetic abilities and has used his vast intellect to create a variety of devices including anti-gravity technology and a telepathy-inhibiting helmet. Quire is proficient in the use of a bullwhip, is a capable ice skater, an avid video game player and wears corrective lenses.

POWER GRID	1	2	3	4	5	6	7
INTELLIGENCE							
STRENGTH							
SPEED							
DURABILITY							
ENERGY PROJECTION							
FIGHTING SKILLS							

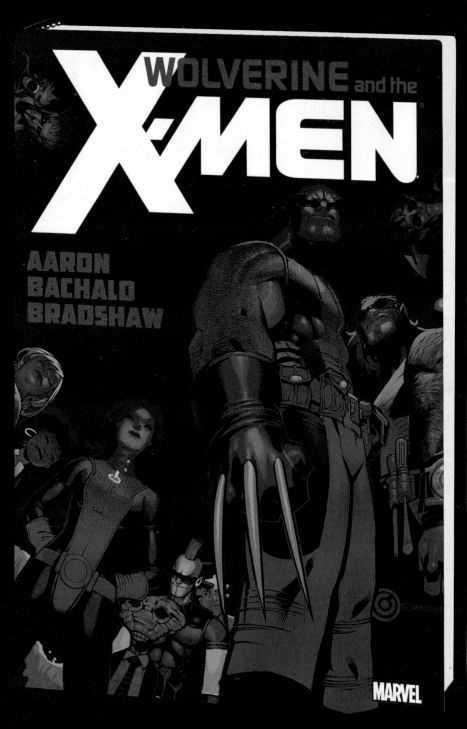